THE LEAST TI

- Stride -

The Least Thing

edited by
Angela Topping

THE LEAST THING

First edition 1989
c. Stride Publications
(copyright reverts to individual authors)

ISBN 0 944669 65 8

Cover image:

'Thy Rosy Cross
Swallowdale, Summer 1987'
by Garry Fabian Miller
Copyright 1989

Published by
STRIDE
37 PORTLAND STREET
NEWTOWN, EXETER
DEVON EX1 2EG
ENGLAND

THE LEAST THING

AN ANTHOLOGY OF CHRISTIANS WRITING

Epigraph

The Song of Caedmon.

And God said:
sing me somewhat, Caedmon.

I would have sung the mullet and whiting
Shoaling at Whitby, the occasional porpoise
that breaks a summer horizon, the pigs
and goats poked into market.
I'd have had men listen
to new songs at harp-passings,
sung the wondrous windwork of gulls.

But God thought otherwise, sold me on dreams:
sing me Creation, Caedmon, the song
that's acceptable, that does me some credit.

So I the uneducated
was saddled with miracle; big words
broke on me, a galeforce of syllables
swept up from nowhere, I would have welcomed
a start nearer home, a local beginning.

But God thought otherwise:
work on my handiwork, carve it on crosses,
sing in Northumbrian the way the world got to
this bleak point of history. Sing to the mindful,
make me some worship.

I would have started the other way round,
charting our wonders, the wonders about us,
the disorder of gulls in a pleasure of words,
the glint of the mullet, the pigness of pigs.

Matt Simpson. from 'Making Arrangements' (Bloodaxe 1982)

Introduction.

I don't like labels, and this anthology doesn't seek to attract them. It does offer a taste of the work of some poets who also happen to be Christians, in whose work the religious and the secular, the concrete and the visionary coexist. Submissions came to me by invitation, both particular and general, and I have simply chosen the poems I thought were the best, in the sense of being well-crafted and accessible. Though diverse, individualistic and written from different denominational viewpoints, they do unite in their striving to express doubt and failure with honesty, and also to celebrate *'the wonders about us'*. The poets are not offering dogma, but exploring their preoccupations within the Christian context.

I have chosen Matt Simpson's poem *'The Song of Caedmon'* as a kind of epigraph because it states what these poems do for me. They make 'a *local beginning'* in praising God, each exploring in its own way *'the disorder of gulls...the pigness of pigs'..*

I want to thank Rupert Loydell for inviting me to edit this anthology. I've worked within his original framework of large selections from few poets. Thank you also to George Szirtes for finding time to write a foreword, and Matt Simpson for giving support and encouragement as well as permission to quote *'The Song of Caedmon'* in full.

Angela Topping

FOREWORD

To compile an anthology of specifically Christian poetry would probably prove a much harder task than this present one of compiling work by poets who are Christian. Since nobody is sure what body of doctrine comprises Christianity any more, and since the Western world has become predominantly secular, the terms of reference themselves have become elusive. It is true that we live in a country that may broadly be described, in the words of Peter Porter, as 'residually Christian', which is to say that people continue to be married in churches, to sing carols and to attend midnight masses. On a deeper level they retain the substructure of Christian - probably Anglican or Nonconformist - ethical assumptions which do not seem to effect their voting habits one way or another (possibly they never did). It may appear that Christianity has become a portmanteau word to cover a multitude - if not of sins - then at least of attitudes, and that in thi s sense the term is almost meaningless, ranging as it does from a vague idea of sacrifice to an even vaguer one of human decency. Doctrine seems to mean agreeing to a form of words without having any clear coherent idea of what those words signify.

Yet there are clearly and obviously people who, as individuals, are Christians, for whom the Christian experience is fundamental. There are those who pray, those to whom the words and deeds of Christ are a spiritual light, those who are cheered by simply hearing the broad magical phrases of the Bible spoken, those who are moved to acts of charity by Christian sentiment, those who feel their blood filled with a peculiar fire when they sip the consecrated wine, those who perceive the world in sacramental terms, to whom the world is, in some Blakean way, a vale of vision.

I don't know which terms the contributors to this volume would choose to describe their own source of faith: their poems must speak for them. Some of the poems spring from Christianity but have no patently Christian context. They may echo a longing for mystical experience, or express a sense of love or loss enriched by Christian attitudes. Peter Walton's poems appear secular in terms of reference but are informed by a sense of childhood or innocence lost. Evangeline Paterson's poems are sometimes in the form of prayer to a God of essential kindliness in the face of large scale human cruelty. Stephen Waling focuses on human relationships and human tragedies.

Specifically Christian subjects seem to insist on more formal structures. A number of poets deal with the Christian story, interpreting it and illuminating it; Brian Louis Pearce searches for significance in the visual world, Anne Ashworth in the homely terms of intimacy, James Harpur in the physical feel of the Biblical and present day world. Elizabeth Black looks at the individual soul, Tony Lucas at social situations and public action. Philip Pacey's poems are addressed to or are about his father: they are borne out of an elegiac feeling for a specific Christian and his character, a loved person. Bruce James is the only poet to take mystical Christianity as his natural subject. In his poems the mystical experience is self contained and seeks no secular context. R.S. Thomas's 'Mass for Hard Times' is the toughest piece of writing and the most naked struggling for faith. It follows the form of the Mass and gains strength from its structure. I think it touches depths that are specifically Christian yet remain deeply moving even for the most fervently atheistic reader.

Christian poetry flourishes best at poles of experience, in those ages where faith is either general or put most severely to trial. It flourishes in Dante and Southwell, in Herbert and Hopkins. There are of course Christian poets in many ages and many cultures, and some of these may be great poets partly because of their Christianity: Blake and Smart allied to madness, Donne and Johnson fixed in their sense and senses.

Mealy-mouthedness and vagueness are the enemies of all great poetry and I am afraid that as far as organised religion is concerned we are living in vague and mealy-mouthed times. It is unavoidable that this collection should show neither a clear pattern nor set a clear example. If only it could give us some idea of a poetry that is both Christian and crystalline. But that, as Angela Topping firmly states, is not its job. Instead it brings together a variety of poems and tells us there is a common denominator at work in them. To locate that common denominator, or spirit, is the task of the reader.

George Szirtes

PETER WALTON

GIFTS OF BREATH

I

The first is quick and hot:
Lovers' or baby's breath
Of blind beginnings.

II

Next comes *andante* breathing, of success;
Ambition realized; the air of smiles.
It asks for nothing more than to go on.

III

But what I most need now is the long inward
And outward thread of control; self-mastery;
Freedom from events; a swift soaring.

AN EASTER VISIT

The wind made sea-sounds in the trees outside
As I lay awake among the sacred
Scarred remembered furniture - stretched

On the loving rack of my care
For parents, children and wife. To share
My worrying-fit the curtains swayed, unsure.

Then the child at my side laughed out loud
In his sleep - sudden and confident and new.

AN END TO PLAYING

It's late. I'm in the bathroom
Towelling off the day
In air that's moist and warm.
Blue curtains are the sky.

Steam blooms the place where play
Has ended - tossing on the sill
A horse, gun-belt and saddle,
And a plastic red necktie.

A pistol and a stetson lie
Two fields of tiles away,
As I track the trail blazed by my boys
Then scan the sill again

And see that the rider's missing -
And think of childhood gone.

BEHIND THE OWL

Every household has this, I expect:
Some place or ornament as anchorage
Against forgetfulness. There lie the slips
Of paper saying pay or go or do,
Or simply keepsakes that have caught the mind.
Ours is a tubby mottled-brown glass owl,
Hunched on a bookcase top. Behind him
Stands a lamp-base bottle, green
And filled with pebbles now to give it weight.
Between these two we put important

Trivia. Here tickets, bills, reminders -
Stacked and curled - accumulate like leaves.
Seasons are spanned in this slim space;
Part history, part living in the future.
The code words are 'behind the owl'
For this untidy press of paper
Nudging the glass bird forward
On his ledge. He stares out ever-present,
Buddha-wise, regardless of our cares.

DWELLING

"Show me a man who cares no more for one place than another,
and I will show you in that same person one who loves nothing
but himself." (Robert Southey)

We live in a Chinese-puzzle house
Whose pieces stack and interlock,
No space to spare: short twisted stairs
Skew between floors; bookcases jut
From walls; the sitting-room's right
Angled, on a wood-clad chimney breast
Up through the middle of the block.
Tight corners cramp our style.
                                    As best
We can we fetter our demands
And count our luck - while visiting sunlight,
Open and straight, slats through the blinds
Bringing clarity at first. But
Soon it climbs across the toys and chairs
In zebra stripes that dazzle us.

We live boxed in - but move in human
And accustomed curves, grooving
The air and rounding corners as if
They were sea-smoothed. Putting my head
Against the chimney wood, at night, I think
I hear the children's voices, younger;
And our younger words, alone. The past vibrates
As we draw away from it, towards
The mystery that, gathering speed, arcs
Back upon itself.
                        I centre
While I can on this first base, sensing
That one day I will stand like this
To take a last long look around,
Before I ice my mind and then forever leave.

THE ALLOTMENTS

The approach was marked a cul-de-sac
As if it led nowhere; and yet, once through
The old rust-gilded green iron gates, the site
Was full of tracks and paths. Admittedly
There was no other main way out; but then,
That morning on official business there,
I had no wish to leave before I'd seen
All that I had to see. And with that done
I lingered on, strangely at home.

The more I stayed the more I saw; not merely
That there were a hundred plots or so, but all
The ways it had become a rooted place.
Sixty years of growth had changed the access tracks
To country lanes, with chest-high privet
(Rose- and bramble-twined) secluding favoured plots.
A stranger looking into them, I thought
Of cottage gardens without cottages:
All else was there - dilapidated sheds;
A pigeon loft (against the rules perhaps);
The odd pot gnome and weather-vane; and rows
And rows of vegetables, green enfilades
Against the surrounding town miraculously
Stopped short there.

Reluctant still, I read the pinned-up
Competition note - almost a local now.
Nearby a leaky stand-pipe hissed,
And dripped into the thirsty cinders.
Its lengths of joined-up hose grass-snaked away
Round corners, through hedge-thickets, over paths;
Back, back towards the heartland I had left.

HOLIDAY GAME : TANYFRON

Within an hour of our unpacking here
A game has been invented - the rules agreed
For every pitch of ball on chimney-wall
And lower roof. The scoring is obscure
But logical, befitting end of boyhood.
I join them. Soon the local kestrel,
Glint of sun on lake, the cooling car,
Are as forgotten as my tense career.
Creation's ease has breezed across the grass
And made this cottage into our good place.

WORRY WIND

I hate gales. They remind me of everything
I haven't done: roof tiles not fixed; painting
Left; fence posts unsecured. I am found out.
I turn in the dark and think of all
Responsibilities. Have I taught
My sons enough, as they grow tall?
Have they the breath of faith? I cannot know.
A squall of sycamore keys rakes the window.
My own life rattles past.

ON THE LAST DAY OF THE YEAR

Three weeks ago the snow first came,
Made magical my stale way home.
I saw umbrellas mushroom white
In minutes, number plates blank out
On cars that slowed down to a speed
Near bearable to walk beside.
All noise was in a muff. The cold
Astonished, took our breath. It killed
A yearling blackbird on the path.
Ice armour-gripped the ground; then, with
The long-drawn thaw, it ridged and furrowed
Like an unearthly field ghost-ploughed.
Eventually water shone
Along the ruts. A strange bleached green
Showed through the ice-pane as it thinned,
Then shrank to separate lenses laid
Across the lawn.
                        And now it's almost gone.
The generous south wind has brought us spring
Before its time. Accept it though, today,
So it can prime that stubborn hoping
Habit of the heart; keep winter's worst at bay.

LAST CHANCE

The swifts are staying late this year;
And after such a summer, too,
Of rain and cold. Perhaps because
Of that, and not despite, they stay
Keening above the southward
Railway line in the grey September
Evening air - much as a man might hope still,
In the wrong place at the wrong time
Of the year, for something more
From life than cold and rain.

BEYOND HOPE

I love failure. There is about it
Something of the salt wind; of wet heather
In November; of three or two leaves only
Left on a birch tree in the rain; something
Of timeless weather. From such can come, rarely
Enough, a gleam, even a warmth, in spite
Of circumstance. And when it does, smiling
Spring itself has nothing to compare.

EVANGELINE PATERSON

A Wish For My Children

On this doorstep I stand
year after year
to watch you going

and think: May you not
skin your knees. May you
not catch your fingers
in car doors. May
your hearts not break.

May tide and weather
wait for your coming

and may you grow strong
to break
all webs of my weaving.

Song For An Innocent

Born with such gentleness as you,
with such a pure and trusting face,
how could I tell you what I knew? -
this world is not your kind of place.

Your candid look, your artless grace
fit you for somewhere else than here.
This world is not your kind of place.
I wish it were. I wish it were.

Occupant Of The Side Ward

Serena, child of God, sits in the side ward,
gropes the air for words, can find none,
grasps at the passers-by, to clutch hands
and touch faces, whimpering her complaint.
Desperate, she frets
to a crescendo, howls like a beast,
and shocks the echoing corridors of stone
with her unspeakable grief.

                                She will not go
silent into that silence. Stones cry out
for her.

                        God, who made her,
write her down in your book. Do not forget her.

Knitting Woman

In her chosen corner she sits. Rivers of knitting
cascade plaining and purling over her lap
winter and summer together. She has her reasons,
knows that sudden contrary August weather
is worse than blizzards in winter, trusts no seasons.

Her young have escaped. She sees them
at large in the world's cold winds. Her anxious care
follows them all by post, in cumbersome parcels,
cabled and striped and ribbed. She knows no ill
that can't be cured in an Aran jacket, or better
endured in a mohair sweater. God
may temper the wind or not, but never
a lamb of hers will ever be caught shorn.

She sits defying hap and circumstance,
weak chests, ill luck, chaos and old night.

She would like to knit the whole world a pullover.

Female War Criminal.

First, we are shown the camp. What a precision
of ordered barracks, what a source of pride -
the upper and the nether millstones turning
to grind out death by night and day. And you, mill-girl,
turned them.

Did you wear an overall, mill-girl? Did you keep
your hands clean?

And then your victims, ranged behind the wire,
standing, looking through the camera's eye
at a world they knew no longer how to speak to.
When you see them now, mill-girl,
do you wish they had shouted, or wept?

Or do you remember, mostly,
putting your feet up when your shift was over?

Now, half a lifetime later, you, in daylight,
sharp-eyed with cunning and despair. Knowing
at last which mills grind surest, what do you hope for?

God has more mercy than even you can need,
but you, with your heart shrunk to a small stone
by shutting mercy out, what would you do
with mercy now?

Would you know, mill-girl,
how to receive it, now?

A LETTER FROM KIEV

...The autumn rains came just as the
ground on which the foundation
for the stadium was to be set had
been   dug   out   and
loosened...loosened...A landslide...
poured down on to the heavily
populated...Podol...
                        Mark Ya. Azbel: Refusenik

Rochele, dearest child, this letter comes
from me, mired so long in an old sorrow,
to you, in your new life, your happy country.

I think of you often, see the fields of grain
from sky to sky, your house a small island,

and would have come by now, to make a life,
feed hens, scour pans, and watch the children grow,

but stayed, to look each sunset towards the height
of Babi Yar, where Hanna and Moishele died,
where their small bones lie,

                        - But listen, Rochele,
do you remember how we angered them? -
old women, obstinate, toiling upward, short
of breath, stubborn of memory, clutching
stones of remembrance in our fists. They tired
of turning us back. 'This is not a place to weep,'
they said. 'We will make it a place to dance.'

I tell you no lie, Rochele. They said so.
A stadium, they said, and a dancing floor.

And so they brought the great machines, to gouge
the hillside out, and then the autumn rains
came down like Noah's flood, and churned that
    ground
into a heaving tide of mud that rolled
down - and the bones, Rochele, the bones

that saw the light again, thighbones, fingers,
skulls - turning over and over, rolling
down on the crowded Podol, shops and streets
and trams, smothering all in thick silence.

I tell you, Rochele, God is not sleeping.
He would not let them dance above our dead.

Send me the ticket, Rochele. I am coming.

Poem For Irina Ratushinskaya

Because of you, little sister,
our thoughts were tethered in Russia
and tugged to get free.

Because of you our days
were striped with shadow
like the floor of your cell.

Girl in tarpaulin boots,
dreaming a cherry-coloured dress,
we shared in your dying.

But you are the indestructible
root of a flower
under the granite.

You moved mountains.
You showed us a way
through stone.

Speak

The microphone hordes advance.
They are brisk and shining. Their words
rattle like hail.

'How do you fell, Mrs. Tyrwhitt,
Mrs. Pentague, Mrs. Blewitt,
now that your son is killed?
Do you want revenge?'

                       We sit
in our cardigans and aprons,
the photograph at our elbows.
We are diffident and slow.

'How does it feel, Mr. Whittaker,
to be disabled?....Mr. Comstock,
to lose your sight? Are you bitter?'

We sit there, turning over
our huge unaccustomed grief.
The words are slow to come.

The microphones insist.
The faceless millions wait.

'How do you feel,
Mr. and Mrs. Golightly,
now that your child is missing?'

What should we say? What
does the beetle say to the wheel,
the worm to the spade? Does the mown grass
speak?

The Bystanders

And what of those
Who see the flower of innocence
Cradled by the hearth
And never listen
For the tread of the iron soldiers
Entering the village street?

And what of those
Who, caught in a web by the flickering
Feet of the spinning bright dancer,
Never listen
For the sound of the sword blades honing
In the yard?

And those who, threading a way through
The many-throated crowd,
Never heed
Whether they shout 'Barabbas'
Or 'Hosanna'?

Truly they have their reward.
They sleep deep and dreamless
During Gethsemane.

Wiser were those kings, once,
Who turned aside for an angel.

and that will be heaven

and that will be heaven
at last   the first unclouded
seeing

        to stand like the sunflower
turned full face to the sun   drenched
with light   in the still centre
held   while the circling planets
hum with an utter joy

seeing and knowing
at last   in every particle
seen and known   and not turning
away

                never turning away
again

STEVEN WALING

FULL IMMERSION

At first plunge
to dream of origins
    going under
    as the sea washes
    life in her lap

atoms shoal through space
to gather here

    and watch
first tread of some
    footed-thing

on land

A second plunge
and the world is
washed clean as
Augeian stables

rocks settle into
themselves as
ice recedes

earth   naked
drips into
lakes rivers seas

as it rises
from flood

At third plunge
water enters
mouth nostrils eyes

          flows
from each orifice
as I rise   then only
will they clothe me
in white
language

            yet
to be spoken

DELIVERY

A jangling of bells in the road
rises and falls away. A white,
reckless ambulance hurls past

the private houses either side,
delivering its parcel
to a red Victorian building

near to the University.
Whilst they post him out of sense
our lives return to harmony;

the world moves back outside
and we return to T.V. sets.
Loaded onto trolleys and

sorted between white sheets,
he's left in pastel rooms
where out of mind is out of sight.

Life drops by him once or twice
to leave him news or bedpans,
or black grapes like postcards
on an aluminium dish.

JOIN WHAT?

If you can't beat'em join'em - but join what?
His eyes see nothing in the gloomy light
of his sitting-room as he considers
the depth of that rhetorical question.

"I've come to see how you're getting on.-"
I manage. Mustn't let it get me down.
Sometimes I feel like I don't want to wake.
"I see." A kind of conversation starts.

And stops. And starts. He shifts in his wheelchair,
grips his white stick like a surrogate life-
If you can't beat'em join'em - but join what?
For two solid years he's kept himself indoors.

I read his bookshelves for a common theme:
two Bibles, thrillers; a sex manual?
Even the mystical books he now can
no longer read are musty with powers

long-worn out. Those pictures on the wall,
ivories collecting dust in the corners,
are giants' toys beside this shrunken man:
If you can't beat'em join'em - but join what?

His life reduced to a chair and a frame
round the loo to hold him as he pees,
I visit him, and find nothing to say
and another fine way of saying it.

He returns to his original question:
If you can't beat'em join'em - but join what?
Like asking the meaning of the universe-
I answer all his problems, walking home.

WORKING NIGHTS

Don't speak
above a whisper

Not a word
from either of you

Creep round the house
and don't flush the lav

You know how your dad
needs them extra winks

and if he wakes
you'll get what for

He's working nights
so's when you go to school

you'll have new britches
and your sister a new dress

So let's play
quiet games, like

Don't bang the door
and Whisper secrets

Let's play mice
with tiny squeaks

but don't wake dad up
when he's just nodding off

you won't like that
one little bit

THE RELATIONSHIP

It was at the end
after coffee and
biscuits that you
introduced yourself.

"Who are you anyway?"
You answered
nothing and I knew
I'd seen you before.

"I remember now."
You turned to the door
as if to say
- You coming, or not?

I didn't want to go
but picked up my coat
from behind a chair
and followed anyhow.

Twelve years since
still on the road
my feet aching and
my tongue hanging out

I still don't know
where we're going to

BRIAN LOUIS PEARCE

from "Heads"

10

April fool's day on
a Good Friday seems
a black joke. Darkness
hangs over the face
of the fool three hours.
The fool hangs. We face
our own darkness, bad
thoughts of the times, God
abandoned, the joke
gone sour in conse-
quence of our folly.

12

Sat on the tomb for our sakes; that's the part
a man can live with. Half explains the smart.

Made the urn flower; fed crowds like Santa Clause.
Rose up as though death's *finis* never was.

Seeing you march straight up to it, the brute
that's still behind mob's clothing, I salute

the tenderness that, like a new recruit's,
was for the Adversary too astute.

Marched up to him, whose malice seemed your equal.
Gave yourself up, to show us the bright sequel.

Do what you've got to. Got to? Quick march. Make
them get on with it for your goodness sake.

They're coming. They make stars go in, that bunch.
About turn, then, as I do in the crunch.

14

You, there,
with your head
craned over the wall,
can you see anything, or
are you just looking?

Cloth-fold
or flowers, gorse;
froth of the almond
dazzle ... No, it's cloud-cold, stone-
shrouded, suddenly.

The sun's
gone in and
all its flowers are an
illusion. I'm not certain.
I can't see a thing.

For love's
sake, here's to
looking. Memories,
words, rug-weft of flowers, are, e-
ven in thought, enough.

15

Desk, Chant,
duties, prayers,
dumb,

I knocked,
you didn't
come.

17

A cheerful courage does not seem enough.
Sheer goodness does not stop it being rough.

My heroine was kind, all would agree,
but the Evil One still took her on his knee.

The Devil, bothered by her kindly heart,
spat twice on it, and tore the thing apart.

The gift of gladness, in her every breath,
gave us new heart, but could not keep back death.

This woman prayed, yet saw no obvious sign.
Others prayed, too. Their grief now joins with mine.

This I can say: her courage did no better
than our lukewarmness, living by the letter,

yet leaves behind itself a fiery charm
which in our faint-heart winter keeps us warm.

Knowing herself the doomed one, still she blessed
the rest of us and gave herself no rest.

Accepting, through necessity, the worst
Satan or man could do, she never cursed

God or her own condition. Like the violet
set by her head, her spririt was inviolate.

Like the buttercups in the meadows of her youth,
her loveliness of spirit is our truth.

The common daisy tells me quite enough.
If there's a heaven, she is of its stuff.

Sudden as fruit parts from the stem
when, ripened, it's ripped from its sphere,
you split in the same peace you grew.

Making shape, although not here,
momently you grow more clear.
Eyes shut, I see you fall from air,

woman, clear-juiced as a pear,
queen-dried, dust-eyed, head culled bare.
Wasp-holoowed, deathly-celled, you wear

the radiance we cannot bear.
The carnal sickness cores the fruit.
The chemistry of evil cuts

away at the original good
of the God we cannot save.
We listen and we shut our ears

knowing we can't ever wave,
say our love, or take your fear
in our hands and make it ours.

19

If
the door to the more
abundant and everlasting
laughter
were to be open for
a few seconds before
it closed for ever,
would you go through?
One might, in a hundred,
and it might be you.

Or
would you hesitate;
be questioning the credentials
of your
informant; say, as hap-
pily most of us may,
it is nice here, we
should like to stay:
as for what's in the new
sphere - well, we don't know:

so
that while you stand weigh-
ing the question, uncertain and
afraid,
the door closes, oppor-
tunity passes and,
more or less burdened,
dog-innocent
yet culpable, you are
left watching the door?

Good Sunday

It's all there at
Marble Hill in
the sun. The shut
door of the tin-

y grotto gone.
Its roof split wide
open to dawn.
God at our side,

on the seat by
the pales, with brack-
en and birds; shy,
glad to be back.

The head still hangs
there, burning in
the heart of flame.
Devil's work, is
it; flame which burns
on the altar,
or fire of sin
that makes the pang?

The fire still burns,
The head still hangs
there, the head is
still bowed (thank God)
to God in prayer.
In the dark night
vocation bangs
the door, head turns.

The door still ratt-
les, the heart still
turns, the head turns
to see who knocks,
jailor or God.
What enters shares
flame to the full,
God, flesh at heart.

ANNE ASHWORTH

REMEMBER JOE?

Aye, I remember. Back in t'north they were,
a building firm. Joe used to sub-contract
to such as me. Mind you, it's many a year
since I came south to t'city. Made a pact,

Joe and I did, whichever were the first
to better hisself would go back and collect
the other, set up business. But I lost

touch with the firm. Joe died, his eldest went
wandering off - went daft, to tell the worst.
Aye, they were joiners really. Not my bent.

Smithing's my trade. I used to make their nails
and iron parts for ploughs - but it were scant
pickings up there. Folk have their share of ills

in city life, but still I'm better off
on government contract. Easy money sales.
See here, this fistful? For supplying stuff

at t'barracks there. Sure, weapons, and why not?
I still do nails. As long as that, and tough,
the ones they want. For executions. Thought

I'd see today's. They say there's one o't'three
from up my part o't'country.
                       Sorry, sport,
I ramble on, not listening. Who d'you say?

Joe's son? Nay, never! Him, d'you mean, as went
daft as a brush? What brought him down this way?
A rabbi? Nay, not Joe's lad. And they don't

crucify rabbis. Well, to think of how
he used to love his timber. Can't account
for folks, now, can you? What a way to go,

with wood and nails. My nails. So what's he done?
Summat as t'Romans don't like t'smell of? Joe! -
glad he can't see the day. Mary's the one

to feel it now. I hardly like to think
they'll use my nails. Nay, if I'd only known...
You feel involved, like. Wouldn't want to link
meself with that. Joe's boy! Could be my son, your son.

MAGI IN OLD AGE

(acknowledgements to T.S. Eliot)

Being skymen, we scarcely knew
how to handle earth, stood awkward at stable door,
entering an uncued scene.
We missed the academe and the ivory tower,
symposium and scented oils.
Blood in the steaming straw:
such elementary biology
stabbed our Achilles heel. Floundering miscast,
no longer knowing how to dispose our hands,
we fumbled the absurd gifts.
In retrospect embarrassment has mounted
to pitch of nausea. Yet how were we guilty?
Foreknowledge of the impossible's not deemed
part of a prophet's kit.
Herod's men knew no better.

What became of the gold? The man his father
was a village joiner; and he, they say, a vagrant
without fixed place or visible means.
A sovereign?
King of the disaffected,
demagogue among dropouts, his royal dimension
unshapes our known mathematics, disconcerts
with new bizarre regalia:
choosing a girded towel for his ermine
and biting briars for bays.
Iconoclast of rule books!
How dared a man beatify the poor?

Gold was irrelevant. But incense
rose to a level of impertinence
clouding the Kingdom's claim.
Why call me good?
he lashed a votary: for none is good
but God. How render, then, this Son of Man,
earth's Everyman and mirror?

Fisher-king, caught in a winding net,
carpenter nailed to his own material,
born among, riding on donkeys,

Most ill-judged
was the aromatic myrrh,
embalmers' sad cosmetic. Here was life
vivid, urgent, precipitate, leaping brooks
and sterile fences in our dormant minds
to win the eternal yes.
Here was a man needed no subterfuge
to petrify decay.
Unitmely urgent
imperious godhead gushed into a garden
while stellar orbits swerved.

And we who traced such trails,
old men in an old myth,
disorientated, dumb in a bare tomb,
our erudition emptied,
as at the borrowed byre, preposterously
abase arthritic knees.

SACRAMENT FOR'SISTERS

Take, eat this body life, this bread,
the daily unremarkable. Here feel
with teeth and fingers stubborn matter's form,
texture of timber, plastic, linen, steel,
the concrete poetry
of earth's variety.
Eat this for Martha. Martha must be fed.
   Lord of the bread, who art
   the wheat germ in the heart,
   let Martha's days
   be praise:
   give us our daily breath.

Drink of this cup. Take willing part
in this Gethsemane. Accept
Love's heartburst. Strain imagination dry.
The vinegar and hyssop sponge reject.
Hope. Wonder. Dare
the groaning prayer.
Drink this for Mary. Mary needs her hurt.
   Lord of the wine, the love
   in which we breathe and move,
   let Mary's pain
   remain:
   give us our daily breath.

OIL OF SPIKENARD

What a spendthrift you are, sir,
a squanderseed wastrel!
Did they never teach you
the puritan virtues?
Look at those puffball heads.
You toss your hair like a petulant schoolgirl, and there -
how untidy you are! - it's like dandruff.
Then there's sperm,
not to mention the sand and the stars and the orange pips.
It's embarrassing, all this extravagance.

And not five minutes ago you painted a skyscape
in a whole fruit salad of pastels,
a study in citrous shades.
So now what are you up to?
You've rubbed it out and started again with blue.
Stop a minute and give us viewing time,
you throwaway artist.
Even when invention funds
are unlimited, surely the waste...

Couldn't this oil of spikenard
have been sold and given to the poor?

PHILIP PACEY

TWELFTH NIGHT

To my father

Tonight I wept for you -
lying beside our youngest, talking of how you
loved to play with them, while you still could
and knew them, and he said it was fun
to visit you, then.

Last night I lit a candle
before our crib, his dinosaur
beside the ox and ass, an Ewok
peering into the manger - aliens
which would not have seemed so to you, either.

Twelfth Night, mourning Christmas
even before it is gone;
mourning you, and much, much more -
your faith my values will not disown -
neither dead nor lost but ailing

MY FATHER AT BRYNMAWR*

Like Paul on the road to Damascus? -
building a swimming pool with out-of-work miners,
a vision of a new world

illumining the middle ground
of the route you had already chosen. And then you too
travelled by sea and land, preaching values

summed up by the one word, Love.
Love, which brooks no compromise, unauthorises
anything but. Not that you used the pulpit

for political ends: even at home, your voting Labour
was a hypothesis you confirmed only
by omitting to deny; we

were to go our own ways, but even now it's as if I betrayed you
the one time I chose to travel First Class,
a long journey, feeling unwell and tempted by the privilege

of not being surrounded. All but impossible to live up to,
your example. if not perfect, is guidance enough.
How flawed is our democracy,
              that you've been disenfranchised by death!

* My father attended a work camp in the South Wales mining
town of Brynmawr, for three weeks in the summer of 1931. Two
years later, in 1933 he sailed to China to work as a missionary.

A PRIEST TO US ALL

for my father

'But he was a priest to us all
Of the wonder and bloom of the world,
Which we saw with his eyes, and were glad'.

Matthew Arnold ('The Youth of Nature')

1

For fourteen years
each week I've slit open your
letter, the folded pages
crackling with humour (who

can make us laugh till
the tears run, and you look on
wondering)

sparkling with observations noted
deftly, in your own words:
unconscious skill I
seek, would inherit

only now knowing (these
years of letters, read
and discarded) what's

lost. Yet, worded in them,
so much of you has passed through me
I've been quickened by
your active consciousness

learned to see
through our seeing through each other's eyes,
reporting back - a name .

on a cab door, on
a greengrocer's box, a potato sack: details
apparently inconsequential, but to us
redolent of place significant

between us. Now this
your latest letter, from a holiday
in the Lake District

telling of a day
of days

I set off at 11.05 a.m.
and by 6.50 p.m. had done
two things which I had
not wanted to be prevented
from doing by timid
temperament or old age...

I walked along the ridge
to the summit of Catbells
which at 1481 feet is
about 300 feet lower than
Pendle...Even so, I did
not feel all that comfortable.

-With no head for heights!
and, tracing your route
in my memory, I recollect
a path narrow
as the ridge-pole of a tent,
Derwent and Newlands pulling
on invisible guy-ropes, and
cropped turf sliding, steep
as canvas.

I met a girl with long
flaxen hair and bright blue
jeans, a picture that goes
on the asset side of the
account.

just when I'm reading - each
night in the halfhour before sleep -
Kilvert's Diary; words
of another clergyman, put down a
a century ago:

...A lovely warm morning so
I set off to walk over the hills
to Colva, taking my
luncheon in my pocket, half a
dozen biscuits, two apples
and a small flask of wine.

Before the chapel house door
by the brookside a buxom
comely wholesome girl with fair
hair, rosy face, blue eyes, and
fair clear skin stood washing
at a tub in the sunshine, up to
the elbows of her round white
lusty arms in soapsuds.

*Out of the corner of my eye
I saw a great light. It was
the heather on Causey Pike
suddenly caught in the sunshine.*

*The Black Mountains were
invisible, being wrapped in
clouds, and I saw one very
white brilliant dazzling
cloud where the mountains
ought to have been. This
cloud grew more white and
dazzling every moment, till
a clearer burst of sunlight
scattered the mists and re-
vealed the truth. The last
cloud and mist rolled away
over the mountain tops and
the mountains stood up in
the clear blue heaven, a
long rampart line of dazzling
glittering snow so as no
fuller on earth can white them.*

My mother's preface:

He is so pleased with his
yesterday's walk that I
must leave him to tell you
about it himself.

3

Your whole life
a sharing and a pointing-out,
unable to bear

that anyone should miss what is theirs to see,
as if Paul
could have taken the wrong turning.

The agony! the frustration!
Reading Kilvert yourself
what fascinated you most in his description of
the 'overwhelming spectacle' was that

*He wanted to draw the cart horse man's attention to it. I had the
same problem with the sun caught heather on Causey Pike. Two
people were coming up the path towards Catbells, their backs
being to the sight. I thought they 'would probably consider me
mad' because distance would have allowed only a waving hand
and my message would not have been clear.*

-If only you had shown the same restraint
on a crowded bus, one summer's day
in Sussex. Having reached the age

of greatest embarrassment, wearing parents
like clothes I couldn't wait to grow out of,
how much rather would I have missed

the sight of a ship leaving Newhaven, than endured
your calling my attention to it, you at one end of the bus
and I at the other and everyone

turning towards *me*. The pain
of wanting to be free, to see
through my own eyes without your prompting -

assiduous spotter of trains, calling out numbers
long after my enthusiasm waned
but I couldn't tell you.

4

Like and unlike you. Failure sparking
irrational rage

eager to share the rare sight of a badger
there! filling the silence where a snuffling was,

striped snout in the light from the caravan,
the two of us stilled by each other's stare

until I broke the spell with a muted call or beckoning
I couldn't make clearer, it mistook for harm.

5

That God was incarnate, taught us to see
seeing through our eyes.

The crux of your vision, which you carried everywhere;
over mountain-trails in Yunnan.

The number of a locomotive you've been calling to me
all my life, I can't or won't make a note of.

A shy creature, frightened off
by the sophistry of modernity.

But your message was clear
and there were many who understood.

1972/1987

'A Methodist minister, my father would never have thought of
himself as a priest in the sense of being a privileged intermediary
between God and other people; his faith was in the 'priesthood
of all believers', and he conceived of his vocation as that of a
servant to believers and unbelievers alike. Interpreted in this
spirit, Matthew Arnold's lines on Wordsworth are very apt.

AN EYE FOR THE GIRLS

Turning you
on your deathbed,
to relieve the pressure points, allow the nurse

to soothe and dress your bedsores.
You're hard to grasp
and we'd not hurt you - slide hands beneath,

clasp wrists and cradle you. You open
your eyes briefly. look at me
for the last time, without recognition -

my first sight of your nakedness
since as a boy I shared your bathwater.
Legs which served you well

bent and emaciated; limp, nearly redundant
genitals. Your son, I've inherited
an 'eye for the girls' - strange

to be virile and human, body and imagination so easily
inflamed, and anything
possible: the slow torture of unfulfilment, drama's

repertoire, the miracle
of procreation. But for you
beauty could not be other than

the radiance and sparkle of soul, a divine
spark, unique, inexplicably whole, glowing
through human form. More potent than reason or morality

how I yearn for faith, spirit, a re-
incarnation to quicken all my seeing
into hallowing.

WRITING HOME

Two years or more since I could write home
knowing my words would make sense to you
and now you're gone

but still, sometimes, particular events
start dictating letters in my mind
specially for you.

Things you would like to know about -
what we get up to, our boys and I
like the two of us used to:

their first League football match;
watching cricket at Fenners
with the odd feeling of having been there with you

but not remembering - drawn to the game partly for your sake
in spite of knowing you could never know.
You were dying, then. No, I don't believe

you're looking down on us now
and yet, as my son said to me years ago
when I'd come back from a distant country,

'I've been talking to you in my memory'.
I'll do the same, I guess, composing
letters to you, whether or not doing so makes sense.

R.S. THOMAS

Mass for Hard Times

KYRIE

Because we cannot be clever and honest
and are inventors of things more intricate
than the snowflake - Lord have mercy.

Because we are full of pride
in our humility, and because we believe
in our disbelief - Lord have mercy.

Because we will protect ourselves
from ourselves to the point
of destroying ourselves - Lord have mercy.

And because on the slope to perfection,
when we should be halfway up,
we are halfway down - Lord have mercy.

GLORIA

From the body at its meal's end
and its messmate whose meal is beginning
                              Gloria.
From the early and late cloud, beautiful and deadly
as the mushrooms we are forbidden to eat
                              Gloria.
From the stars that are but as dew
and the viruses outnumbering the star clusters
                                 Gloria.
From those waiting at the foot of the helix
for the rope-trick performer to come down
                              Gloria.
Because you are not there when
I turn, but are in the turning.
                     Gloria.
Because it is not I who look,
but I who am being looked through
                        Gloria.
Because the captive has found the liberty
that eluded him while he was free
                     Gloria.
Because from the belief that nothing is nothing
it follows that there must be something
                              Gloria.
Because when we count we do not count
the moment between large and small
                        Gloria.
And because, if we are overcome,
we are overcome by nothing
                        Gloria.

CREDO

I believe in God
the Father (Is he married?)
I believe in you the almighty.
who can do anything
you wish. (Forget that irony
of the imponderable.) Rid, therefore,
(if there are not too many
of them) my intestine
of the viruses that against
(in accordance with? Ah, horror!)
your will are in occupation
of its defences. I call
on you, as I have done
often before; (Why repeat,
if he is listening?) to show
you are master of secondary
causation. (What have physics to do
with the heart's need?) Am I
too late, then, with my language?
Are symbols to be in future
the credentials of our approach?
(And how contemporary
is the Cross, that long-bow drawn
against love?) My questions
accumulate in the knowledge
it is words are the kiss of Judas
that must betray you.

              (My
parentheses are exhausted.) Almighty
pseudonym, grant me at last,
as the token of my belief,
such ability to remain
silent as is the nearest to a reflection
of your silence to which
the human looking-glass may attain.

SANCTUS

The bunsen flame burns and is not consumed,
and the scientist has not removed his shoes
because the ground is not holy.

And because the financiers' sun
is not Blake's sun, there is a
word missing from the dawn chorus.

Yet without subsidies poetry
sings on, celebrating the heart
and the 'holiness of its affections'.

And one listens and must not listen
in vain for the not too clinical
sanctus that is as the halo of its transplanting.

BENEDICTUS

Blessed be the starved womb
and the replete womb.

Blessed the slug in the dew
and the butterfly among the ash-cans.

Blessed be the mind that brings forth good and bad
and the hand that exonerates it.

Blessed be the adder among its jewels
and the child ignorant of how love must pay.

Blessed the hare who, in a round
world, keeps the tortoise in sight.

Blessed the cross warning: No through road;
and that other cross with its arm out, pointing both ways.

Blessed the woman who is amused
at Adam feeling for his lost rib.

Blessed the clock with its hands over its face
pretending it is mid-day, when it is mid-night.

Blessed be the far side of the Cross and the back
of the mirror that they are concealed from us.

AGNUS DEI

No longer the Lamb
but the idea of it.
Can an idea bleed?
On what altar
does one sacrifice an idea?

It gave its life
for the world? No,
it is we give our life
for the idea that nourishes
itself on the dust in our veins.

God is love. Where
there is no love, no God?
There is only the gap between
word and deed we try
narrowing with an idea.

JAMES HARPUR

Christ and the Woman of Samaria

I can remember it now:
The milky turquoise sky,
The pervasive summer heat,
The sheep cropping the grass.

I meandered up the slope;
The stillness held every visible
Stone and shrub in place,
And far away in another valley
There came the gentle clonking
Of a cowbell as it dangled
In rhythm with a warm animal body.

My life had become as empty as
The water-jug I was carrying,
As stale as the distant walled town
With its gossip, sex and intrigues.
But the air was clean
And a stream was cleansing its pebbles.
My blue silk gown was absorbing warmth.

I didn't notice him at first,
For he was sitting by the well,
Dressed in the colour of a faded rose,
Half obscured by the trunk of a tree.
He asked for water
For though his eyes were moist
His lips were dry
And when he spoke,
The words seemed to lodge themselves
Deep within the back of my head —
What I said in reply seemed silly quibbling
But he didn't interrupt,
He just looked inside me to the bitter
Shrivelled root inside my breast.

'God is a spirit' he said, and drew
An arc with his finger around his head;
And I knew what he meant,
Knew I had lived this moment before,
As if the glowing elements of a forgotten dream
Were tumbling out into the waking world;
I told him that I knew the Christ would come
To impress upon him my belief.
He smiled and it was then I realised
Who it was, who this strange man was:
I felt a sudden stirring and wrenching within
And then a tight tug in my stomach rising
As if water were being drawn
Right up inside the darkness of my body
Into the dazzling blue light.

The Magi.

Down in the desert,
Three camels clinked through sand
Shimmering like frost
From the stretching dunes of stars
That, as if a glass dome had shattered,
Were sprayed
Frozen still in their fall.

Three Persian pilgrims,
For three days drifting homewards,
One by one by one,
Linked by a silence come
From Bethlehem.
Amidst the breath of cow and ox
Milking the straw-filled air,
Their brains chattering with hope
Were brought to silence
As a crisis cry for life
Broke from the mother's breast,
And shivered their spinal cords.
Sheepishly they laid their gifts,
Glittering, rare and pungent,
Amongst the crusted stable opulence,
And left, unable to conjure
A word of wisdom or wit.

Down in the desert,
Three camels clinked through sand
Shimmering like frost
From the stretching dunes of stars,
Now fading like magic
Before the pastel, golden east
And the wakening red raw dawn,
Yawning out its giant cry.

Messiah

The wind shivered the olive trees
Into a shimmer of whispers,
And smears of muck proclaimed His coming
On all the whitewashed walls.
Jerusalem was ready.
We waited, as for centuries,
For the clouds to dim the sky
And gauze the sun to an opalescent moon;
And silent lightning crickling the horizon—
A crack and the sky shorn
With a gash of inflooding light,
Our lungs sucking in our ribs
And the flaming gold chariot blazing nearer,
Horses white and flinting out sparks,
Their ruby eyes flashing blood
Tails ripping loose in the wind;
And the god of our hopes,
At last quenching our ancient prayers,
Coming to save us in a glory of light
Softening in strata and cloaking
The diamond core of his body;
His features too far to be seen
Yet erupting behind our eyes,
His glowing flesh melting and reforming,
Our hearts bursting like trumpets,
Our ears spiralled deaf by the winds
Blowing our enemies off the earth...

When the rabbi waddled up the street
On a dung-discharging donkey,
Our hopes fell one by one
Like the palms dropping before him.
We slunk off and got drunk.
One of us was sick standing up.
Our blood frets.
I can't get to sleep
The pulse is pumping so loud in my brain.
Change is in the air.
I try to sleep counting dead Romans.

At the Temple of Jerusalem

A bloated sun burns the desert world to rust,
Diminishing heat shimmers over dust,
Throats are granulated by the grit,
Flies glint on scabs of donkey shit;
Warm and goaty smells thickened with disease,
Gloat through streets sealed off from any breeze.
Indoors, a dog drops out its lathered tongue,
And acid words are breathed by stale lungs.

Next day, a billion fires cleanse the east,
It is the last day, the great day of the feast;
Empty barren minds, the muttering plotting crowd,
Stand stunned as they hear him cry aloud
Words simpler than they could possibly think,
Bottomless words from which they cannot shrink:

'If any man thirst, let him come unto me and drink.'

Lindos, Rhodes: the landing of St Paul

He steps ashore; the sun is at its peak.
Was it chance or fate that brought him to this place?
What bastard patois would the natives speak?
What sacred words would the Holy Spirit
Cause to pour from his animated face?
What weighted stones would fly at him like spit?

Fresh water and meat were turning in the minds
Of his men, sunburnt, taciturn with a violence
Turned inward to the gut. At least the winds
Had blown themselves into a gentle breeze.
No man, no bird, no cricket broke the silence
As he gave thanks, palms open, on his knees.
    And still Rome, invisible as a magnet,
    Was drawing him closer with every sunset.

Prisoners of Conscience Window
Salisbury Cathedral

Their disembodied heads float
Below the underwater blue
That flows from the glass mosaic,
Their eyes from which flies hope
Are raised high in helpless horror.
Their mouths hang agape in a silence
That caresses the air like a web.
If ever this glass did crack
And the blue shards dropped
Hissing like sheet ice,
What hot cries, frozen stiff
In their brickle throats,
Might bloody the air,
The outbursting outrage
Of those shattered by suffering,
By unadorned sickening despair.

In the centre, the Redeemer,
In whose agony the panes are steeped,
Is lit and relit on the cross
As daily the soft dawn seeps up
Into his brittle and broken body,
Thawing out the gagged cry
'Eli, Eli, lama sabacthani?'
It rises, fills the other eyes
That had escaped in sleep
The glazed stare of those
Who would torture out submission
In the holy cause of lies and fear.

But now at nightfall,
After a day of being fired to life,
They become once more extinguished
In the gloom of the lancet windows,
Consigned to the cycles of light and dark
Till resurrected on the last day,
The blue membrane of glass
Rent like the veil of the Temple,
And the prisoners for truth coming forth
Blackened before the blaze of sun.

Myth

The snake lay still, the essence
Of snake generations compressed
Into each atom of nerve and muscle;
Its oily green coils glistening
With the dryness of glazed paint.

The warm-blooded serene saint
Leant over and let drip drops of holy water
Until like a fork of lightning spasm
The snake, crucified, spat and spat
Back the gospel with hiss and venom,
Its blind tongue flickering foil-like,
Head and tail split from each other
By the great sackweight of solid flesh.
Unpeeling itself, it began to shudder,
Then rocketed through the bracken
That crackled like rain on a live rail.

Wherever he went, the snakes vanished:
He lobbed a cross,
They darted into foxholes.
He clicked his fingers,
They slipped between the cracks of gravestones.
He mouthed 'Abracadabra',
They melted into their own mirages.

But while the saint kicked off his sandals,
The snakes chewed their way through thick earth,
And they met, and snake ate snake
Until just one serpent, sweating in its juices,
Its back crusted with the hills of Ireland,
Lay still.

And now it lies waiting,
Swelling under the thin skin
Of the New Testament,
Waiting for the saints on St Peter's
To drop off, one by one

Like stand-up ducks at a rifle range.

BRUCE J. JAMES

The Body-Tree

This Body-Tree

    Is Bonded with The Womb

Of All that ever can be called

    Human

The Stark-Oak Winter

    Bark of Piercd Frost

Has melted from Its frozen tomb

    As Brother

The Razed Tear of Thorns

    Low, Blood - Hung

Is Risen from this World

    On Crown-formed

        Altars.

For, as The Root

    Of The Divine

Drives Child-Warm Pleasures

    To Its Soil

No Feast-Spoils of Bread and Wine

    Harm The Keeper's Joy

At Pruned Branches of Our

    Present, Past and Future.

Mater Redemptis

All the sorrows of His universe
have torn into my breasts,
yet my milk flows to feed the multitudes
without regret.

I was born without sin, and crushed
the head of the serpent beneath my feet;
the stars in the heavens act as my crown,
and my girdle is the strength of the beauty
of all truths.

I shall not desert you in your final days,
nor shall I forget you in mid-summer;
as the blossoms of May come every season
so shall my love for you last into eternity;
in the winter of darkness I shall be as a light
as in a harbour in the fiercest storm.

I shall be known
throughout all ages
for my humility.

My motherhood
shall blanket you,
feed and comfort you,
as though I were a star
rising in your breast.

In the midst of misfortune
I shall raise you out of your solitude
and place you amongst your brethren,
the children of the light eternal,
who shall guide your hands and feet
to freedom in my land.

As the wanderer
sets out upon his journey
I shall be before you
with the lamp of my virginity
ahead of you as your light.

All mankind shall see the day
He comes together with me;
there is no escaping
my maternal solicitude.

I am guardian and shepherdess,
and cleanse you in my mill of love,
grinding your soul into ears of wheat
from which you shall create
the bread of men and angels
and my song shall cultivate your will.

As I rise as the morning star
you shall be justified before me;
I shall bury your bones and flesh
to grist them in tune for paradise
when you do not expect it, and have
given up all hope of glory to come.

I shall water the rocks and lilies
with my tears so that you shall be cleansed;
you shall be called blessed and righteous
even though you have sinned,
for I shall ask for and gain your forgiveness.

So listen and hear my voice -
it is as pure as the snowcloud
over Judah, and it bears fruit
in the lowest and in the loftiest of places.

Be meek before me and I shall
tender your redemption;
my consolation is the source
of all your love.

I sing in the mountains
of my blessedness,
and all nations shall call me holy.
You were born to share the peace
of the dove, for there is no one
but the spirit that leads you to me,
so that you might name me
the handmaiden of the Lord Almighty

I am given the motherhood of man,
and I shall never forsake the humble;
I shall seek no retribution against the sinner
who loves me, for the mouth of the Lord
has spoken, and mighty is His Name.

ELIZABETH R. BLACK

Summer Delirium

Torn in this heat
between desire and self effacement
I talk to sparrows,
lose myself in a hollow house.

So many thin dark halls
so many shady rooms
so many withered smiles
so many torn curtains in
half breezes.
Over the floor
a centipede runs.

>*Show me the proper door,*
>*my fingers are raw knocking!*
>*Show me the proper earth,*
>*my knees are scabbed stumbling!*
>*Show me the proper sky,*
>*I am delirious searching!*
>
>*I am summer's dove*
>*crying,*
>*but you do not listen!*

My soul speaks to me:

>You say you don't understand,
>you say you are perplexed.
>As day unravels,
>wanders to dusk,
>you know you do understand,
>secretly,
>because you have been
>here before.

Then comes night,
the huge white moon
too close.

Fall Song by the River

At river's side
we part:
too many spoiled years,
our souls on fire.

Will I yet live
with all the sorry winds
wandering here?

Tell me one day
we can die together.

Already we begin,
you and I,
hand in hand
by the river.

Now the wind fans
your thin hair,
speaks to us
of what we could have been.

Now the wind falls.
Do you feel me dying
into your hand
where I always longed to be?

Late day darkens,
light dies.

Now leave me,
alone in blue
among the fallen leaves.

Songs of a Young Schizophrenic

1

I am a silent mockingbird
mimicking worlds
in and out of time.
I lose myself,
sometimes never find myself.
I pawn myself for a nickel lie,
a shoe string.
Sometime on a summer night
look to my lit window
I am up late
trading in the air
for sighs,
asking stars
for friendship.

2

I am a quiet day:
   mist
   brown leaves fallen
   a lonely dandelion.

My doors,
silent and vacant,
stare,
wondering.

My sun bleeds
pain and hope.

My winds are heavy,
come from far:
   life of a lost time,
   a sea,
   a shore,
   birth of a bitter change.

My winds veer.
   I fear—
then
   relapse

to the strange other day
I sometimes know.

She opens and closes
my doors.
So much silence
where winds turn
in yellow mist.

3

I am dead
my shadow
moves
breathes
writes

But talk of a
heart
lungs
soul
I come up
short

Only a river
all the uncertainty
of water
one white bridge
to nowhere

Do not call me
I may turn my head
but my eyes are glass
my tongue is crystal
my bones are lead

Sing into winds
as I do now
regretting what is past

TONY LUCAS

No.EL

The word was made flesh
and marked as a statistic
in the imperial register:
- one more birth,
one more indigent,
displaced and homeless,
soon another refugee.

A figure that did not add up,
like an odd half penny
carried on, persistent,
a marginal intruder,
later becoming one more
unemployed, a native
vagrant and religious
dissident, altogether
one more suspect,
source of agitation,
trouble-maker.

An awkward number that recurred,
annoyingly defiant,
breaking the order of the columns,
till there was only one resort
which was to cross the number out
and cancel its existence.

The which was promptly done,
correctly justified, except
the number would not go;
it reappeared and multiplied,
defying ruler and eraser,
threatening the bases of security.

Eventually,
for the sake of clear accounting,
a whole new mathematics was
devised around this figure
to contain it. Even then
it would get out of hand
from time to time,
upsetting calculations.

Such numerology now
smacks of an unprogrammed age,
long shut within the safety
of old ledgers. But as
the needle jumps awry,
and the unscheduled blip
cavorts across the screen
to crumble theory in
a hundred questions, we
may guess God's awkward number
dances still, upon
the data bank and through
the circuits of computers,
to defy our certainties,
and unbalance the account;
a shift of the horizon
that will nag at tidy minds
the way a crying child
may nag a restless night.

TOWER BLOCK

The Council's plywood barricades
block up the frames where wired glass
was systematically smashed out.

Wet stains that pattern the bare
concrete walls, are covered up
by over-lapping spray-gun scrawls,

proclaiming loyalties and hates,
initials, names, the brute
ideograms of failing speech.

Inside the battered lifts a stench
of disinfectant still insinuates
those smells its wash has drowned.

Press on the broken button,
or climb up the glass-strewn stairs,
along the cloned, deserted landings

bolted doors conceal the warmth of homes,
the pride of fitted carpets,
comforts of a frayed armchair, and

families as alive to laughter or to pain
as those behind herbaceous borders,
safe along the neat suburban lanes.

ONE WHO KNOCKS

He is the one keeps knocking at my door,
begging the price of lodging, of a meal,
a ticket to his family in the north.
As much as I am moved to help him, I
am held back by distrust, the chance
it may encourage him to try for more.

He is the one whose giro hasn't come;
who has no heating and no food at home.
I quite believe him; then again, I don't.
He swears that, faithfully, he will repay
on Tuesday. I know he won't, but also
guess he really means the promise now.

He is the one, disguised by drink, wanting
a sandwich, red face, mumbling unlikely offers
to 'come back again and do some work'.
I butter bread compliantly, glad
of the simple, quick response to needs
that I could not begin to try and meet.

He is the one who wastes my time with his
rococo strategies and rambling tales,
resisting all attempts to reach a point.
A fiver soon seems cheap to buy back half
an hour: but is it money or the company
he wants? He couldn't answer that, nor I.

Sometimes I see him through the spyhole
- the dirty coat, wild hair and manic eye;
tiptoeing down the hall in silence, I plead
the urgency of work, of rest, of fear,
leaving him there to knock. He leaves me
stripped quite bare of every lame excuse.

And if he grows abusive when I'm curt,
unhelpful, it is the distorting mirror for
my moods: his angry impotence reflects
them back. Ever the outcast he confronts
all my belonging. No accusation, no
good work, is going to earn an easy peace.

VESPER

Voices at play carry across the water;
the sun drops by St Mary's tower.

Under the cloudless evening sky
boats swing at anchor. But as I lie here
on the deck, the book I'm reading sets up
its echoes of Cold War; and from the cabin
I hear snatches of the television news,
the cries of children with no future.

Last night I lay awake at four o'clock
having to calm the usual fears.
The lake is quiet now, and free from storms;
fish plop in the darkness -
all you need do is cast a net...
...*from sudden death, Good Lord, deliver us.*

The stillness is so fragile,
and we injure it with every move we make.
Yet it survives, and will outlast us
to come creeping back, together with the weeds
that reclaim everything we turn our backs on.
The wilderness shall blossom and be glad.

Later, with our loving,
we shall rock this boat.
May God defend us from the prophet's crime
of crying 'Peace' where there is none.
Keep me as the apple of an eye:
Hide me under the shadow of your wings.

After the day's heat
we wait for cool night rain.

IN THE NEXT DARK AGES

In the next Dark Ages – they will
    sack our factories for building brick,
    put metal wheels and plastic sprue to new
    ingenious uses in their low technology,
    and keep components of computers for
    adornment or as counters of exchange;

                        – sites of
    nuclear installations, long abandoned,
    will be wreathed in mists of legend and
    avoided like the plague, for fear of all
    those sickly curses baneful ghosts who haunt
    their precincts work on wanderers straying near.

In the next Dark Ages – thieves will
    bash old ladies for their margarine tubs,
    yoghurt pots, collected coffee jars;
    and magistrates will wonder how we walked
    the streets unarmed, yet let our children wreck
    appliances that they cannot replace;

                        – men will
    marvel at the things we take for granted,
    like good drains and plumbing, plastic bags,
    elastic, neon lights and nylon string;
    that every neighbourhood has doctors, schools,
    and shops supplying almost everything.

In the next Dark Ages – monks and
    scholars of new righteousness will scorn
    the degredation of our taste, yet file
    rock music and old films within their libraries;
    while Chinese connoisseurs prize packaging
    and adverts as our peak of fine design;

                        – they will
    often tell how God's wrath finally was
    visited on us judgement for our
    wealth and waste, our greed and indolence,
    corruptions of our skill and power; yet still
    they'll envy us our life, our golden time.

TOTAL ECLIPSE

(The next total eclipse of
the sun, visible from London,
will be in the year 2142)

I shall not see it,
nor the last child born,
nor even yet his son.
Still it will happen,
This is a calculation
you can count on; not
like the railway timetable
that can be disrupted,
cancelled, or run late.

It does not need us,
and we cannot interfere.
If, by that time,
there should be no one
left alive down here
to witness, even so
it will take place.

And knowing this we are
at once diminished, yet
at the same time strangely
reassured, - stirred by
the synchromesh of cosmic
gears, as if believing
what has order must have
purpose, - as if we sensed
the music of the spheres.

VIGIL FOR PEACE, BRIXTON, SUMMER 1981

Only the usual handful of embarrassed christians
standing around, not sure how obviously
they should appear to pray —

eyes up, eyes down, — whether to grin at friends
who nudged late into the circle,
wondering how to rise above

the roar of evening traffic round the island.
Somehow the policemen made it seem worthwhile —
a large green busload, brought in from the suburbs,

just in case the sisterhood had hidden half-bricks
in their handbags, or the charismatic clergy
turn from tongues of fire to petrol bombs.

But while, across the road, they played
at cards or dozed, our silence deepened.
Candles were lighted all around the rosebed.

Passing children who stopped by to stare
were caught up, sharing a curious quiet.
So, the evening darkened; street lamps

turned the trees to yellow, candles brightened
and the silence grew; until the chiming
of the Town Hall clock plumbed through

and people turned to shake hands,
talk a little, then walk quietly away,
— not wanting to claim anything,

but just returning through scarred streets,
past shops sold up and gone, leaving the idle bus
to drive its bored young men back home.

AT THE CELL OF MOTHER JULIAN

No one can kiss the ground she knelt on,
lift a flake of plaster
where she might have pressed her head.

It would be fine to think
that it was some good providence obliges us
to use our own imagination and her words instead.

The place has been rebuilt from dereliction;
long centuries of neglect were detonated
with a blast bomb in the war;

now an etched lamp hangs as the only decoration,
making a shadow of the bare stone altar
dance across the cork-tiled floor.

Here is no gilded clutter, fusty relics,
clouding the straight plainness of her shrine;
no painting of her life in stilted tableaux.

The kind of visitors who find their way seem
mostly those who come to share a stillness,
sense a presence, hear an echo of her prose.

They leave behind a litter of torn paper,
tattered scraps, fixed to a notice-board,
each bearing its request for prayer, —

pinned on her promise that "All shall be well",
— as if this truly were an anchorage
where battered hopes might look for some repair.

A life dropped into silence,
but to such depth of vision that the ripples
never ceased to spread,

and now their wash returns to this still centre,
bringing searchers: after what? — a living cell,
some kind of resurrection from the dead?

SACRAMENTAL

There must have been a time for him to ponder
on what pledges could be given when he left;
which tokens would be best to carry the assurance
they were in his presence always, not bereft.

Did he consider kindly milk? Or water,
pure sustainer of each thing that lives?
Might soft ripe fruit or soothing oil make signs?
Or else the sweetness that the honey gives?

But three long years of conflict, finding fault,
all the cheap jibes, the lies, had gone before;
layers of cynicism and deceit,
showing a murderous hatred at the core.

So, in the end, he said: "Here is your crust,
the bread for want of which you'd cheat and kill, −
the daily loaf, for which you sweat and scrape, −
take it for free, to break and eat your fill.

"Here is the wine that can untie the knots
of your suppressed desire, and make you mad;
the cup of your wild truths, your passions, fears, −
take this between you, drain it, and be glad.

"Refine and spiritualise them as you may,
they will remain coarse signs for all to read:
make no demands on talent, wit or wisdom,
yet still meet you at the desperate roots of need.

"These will endure, withstand you, and proclaim
− though each dig down as deep as they may please −
'He has been here before you, and his life
was broken, poured out, and consumed − as these.' "

Contributors

Matt Simpson's new collection, *'Elegy for the Galosher Man'* is due from Bloodaxe in 1989.

George Szirtes' most recent collection is *'Metro'* (Oxford Poets 1988).

*   *   *   *

Peter Walton was born in 1936 in Essex, grew up in the West Midlands and now lives in Cheshire with his wife and two sons. He read geography at Cambridge and now works as head of a Department of the Environment. He appeared in the anthology *'Poetry from Cambridge'* (1958), and has since published in a variety of magazines. He was a prize-winner in the 1981 BBC National Poetry Competition and has broadcast on a number of occasions. His 1977 collection *'Out of Season'* (Carcanet) won a North West Arts publication award. Currently he is marketing a novel and planning a second poetry collection. A convinced Christian since University days, he describes himself as an 'Anglican Existentialist'.

Evangeline Paterson was born in Ireland and lives in Leicester. She is married to a Professor of Geography and has three children. She is editor of the magazine *'Other Poetry'*. Her latest collection is *'Bringing the Water Hyacynth to Africa'* (Taxvs 1983).

Steven Waling was born in 1958 in Accrington. A Theology graduate, he lives in Manchester where he is editor of *'Four Eyes Press.'* His first pamphlet was *'The Long Way Round'* (1987). His second pamphlet *'Riding Shotgun'* is being published as a result of The Poetry Business Pamphlet competition and is back to back with Michael Lasky's *'Cloves of Garlic'.* He has recently launched the magazine *'Brando's Hat'*.

Brian Louis Pearce was born in Acton, London in 1933. He is a former college librarian, and was in the R.A.F. from 1951-53, carrying coals. He is a lay preacher, an Elder U.R.C. and has served as chairman of Twickenham Christian Council. He has a deep involvement in literature, being a writer, lecturer, editor, tutor in Creative Writing, writer in schools etc. His many publications include novels, stories, poetry (including a Selected Poems). He has contributed to many journals as well as PEN and Arts Council anthologies.

Anne Ashworth lives in Blackpool where she is librarian at a sixth form college, also teaching poetry there. She is a radical-heretical Christian, belonging to the United Reform Church. Her work has appeared in many poetry magazines and she is reviews editor of *'Reform'*. Her second collection of poems is due shortly from Littlewood Press.

Philip Pacey, born in 1946, is Arts Librarian at Lancashire Polytechnic. A recipient of a Gregory Award, his published collections include *'Charged Landscapes'* (Enitharmon 1978) and a cycle of poems on the lift of Christ, *'If Man'* (Taxvs 1984). His latest book is a Selected Poems, *'Earth's Eye'* available from Stride. He is the son of a Methodist Minister, and describes himself as 'an agnostic with loose connections with the Society of Friends'. He is married, with two children.

R.S. Thomas was born in 1913 in Cardiff. He was educated at St. Michael's College, Llandaff, and University College, Bangor. In 1936 he was ordained as Clergyman in the Church of Wales, retiring in 1978 after working as rector and then vicar in many Welsh parishes. His first collection of poems was published in 1946 and was followed by many others; a Selected Poems was published in 1973. He has also edited various anthologies, including *'The Penguin Book of Religious Verse'* (1963) and selections from other poets including Edward Thomas.

James Harpur was educated at Trinity College, Cambridge and now works as a freelance writer and editor in London. His poetry has been published in numerous magazines and anthologies. In 1985/6 he was the recipient of a Gregory Award. He was a contributor to *'The Official Halley's Comet Handbook'* (1986), editor of *'Great Events of Bible Times'* (1987) and co-author of *'The Atlas Of Enchanted Places'* (1989).

Bruce J. James was born in 1939 in Pembroke Dock, Dyfed. He is a retired Technical Author and lives in Hertfordshire. He is a Catholic, and a member of Ver Poets and The Focolare Movement. He has published two pamphlets, *'Conversations with a lady'* (1987) and *'The Four Temples of Aspiration'* (1988). His poems have been published in a number of magazines including *'Ambit'* and *'Essex Countryside'*.

Elizabeth Rachel Black lives in the States. She studied English at University in England, and now teaches.

      *   *   *   *

Angela Topping was born in Widnes in 1954, was educated at Liverpool University and now lives in Cheshire with her husband and two small daughters. A committed Christian, she belongs to the Catholic Church. She is a Creative Writing Tutor, poet-in-schools and reviewer. Her first collection of poems *'Dandelions for Mothers' Day'* was published by Stride in 1988.

Acknowledgements

Acknowledgements are due to the following magazines and anthologies in which some of the poems first appeared:

To REFORM for Anne Ashworth's poems; to THE MOORLANDS REVIEW for *'At the Temple of Jerusalem'*, ORBIS for *'Messiah'* and THE NATIONAL POETRY COMPETITION PRIZEWINNERS ANTHOLOGY (1979) for *'Myth'* by James Harpur; to CHRISTIAN for *'One Who Knocks'*, *'At the Cell of Mother Julian'* and *Sacramental'*, POETRY SOUTH EAST 1 (ed. Howard Sergeant) and CHRISTIAN for *'No.EL '*, DANCE TO A DIFFERENT DRUM (ed. James Berry) for *'Tower Block'*, SOUTH COAST POETRY JOURNAL (California) for *'Vesper'* POETRY NOTTINGHAM for *'In the Next Dark Ages'*, POETRY REVIEW for *'Total Eclipse'*, LAMBETH ARTS MAGAZINE for *'Vigil For Peace'* by Tony Lucas; to SECOND AEON for selections from *'A Priest to us all'* by Philip Pacey; to STAND for *'Letter from Kiev'*, ORBIS for *'A Wish for My Children'*, LION BOOK OF CHRISTIAN POETRY for *'and that will be heaven'*, the anthology CHAOS OF THE NIGHT (Virago) for *'Female War Criminal'* by Evangeline Paterson; to ORE, REFORM and STRIDE for sections from *'Heads'* by Brian Louis Pearce; to THE POETRY BOOK SOCIETY ANTHOLOGY 1987-88 (ed. Gillian Clarke) for *'Mass for Hard Times'* by R.S. Thomas; to THE GREEN BOOK for *'The Allotments'*, SMOKE for *'Dwelling'* by Peter Walton.